Angel,
The Couch Potato

Written by:
Donna Dobroski

Angel, The Couch Potato
Copyright © 2022 by Donna Dobroski

All rights reserved. No part of this publication may be reproduced, distributed, or transmitted in any form or by any means, including photocopying, recording, or other electronic or mechanical methods, without the prior written permission of the author, except in the case of brief quotations embodied in critical reviews and certain other non-commercial uses permitted by copyright law.

Tellwell Talent
www.tellwell.ca

ISBN
978-0-2288-5832-4 (Paperback)

Dedication

To my grandchildren Abigail, Paige, Jacob, J.T. and Joey.

To all the children I had the privilege to teach and read to throughout my wonderful career with the HWCDSB.

Nana has a dog.
Her name is Angel.
Angel is a white dog.
Angel likes Nana's red couch.
Angel lays on Nana's red couch.

Angel likes to eat.
Angel likes treats.
Angel gobbles up her food.
Angel has bad manners.

Angel likes cucumbers.
Cucumbers make Angel fart.
Angel stinks.
Phew!

Angel likes to sleep.
Angel snores.
Angel snores loudly.
Often her snores wake up Nana.

Sometimes Angel has bad dreams.
She howls in her sleep.
Nana wakes Angel up and pets her.
Angel feels better and goes back to sleep.

Angel likes to go for walks.
She smells the grass.
She smells the flowers.
She smells the trees.
She smells the fire hydrants.
She smells the hydro poles.
She smells other dog's backsides.
"Oh, Angel.
That's gross!"

Angel doesn't like rain.
Angel doesn't like snow.
Angel doesn't like when it's too hot.
Angel doesn't like when it's too cold.
Angel likes when it's just right.

Angel likes children.
She likes to visit Abigail and Paige.
She likes to visit Jacob, JT and Joey.
They are Nana's grandchildren.
But mostly, Angel likes to be on the couch.

Angel is Nana's best friend.
They watch TV together.
They sit on the couch together.
They cuddle on the couch together.
They share treats together.

Angel is a couch potato.
Nana is a couch potato.
Angel loves Nana just the way she is.
Nana loves Angel just the way she is.
Together they are perfect couch potatoes!

Acknowledgement

Deanna Maerz, founder of Angel Animal Rescue Foundation (AARF) who brought Angel and her mother Baby Girl into my life.

Much appreciation and gratitude go out to dear friends who helped me complete this first book:

Paula Kent Kuchmey for her encouragement and editing skills.

Trish McDonald for her patience and computer skills.

www.ingramcontent.com/pod-product-compliance
Lightning Source LLC
LaVergne TN
LVHW070047070526
838200LV00028B/415